MW01593464

Opened:
God's Promises of Healing

Heidi Hunt

ISBN-10: 1717582710
ISBN-13: 978-1717582713

DEDICATION

This book is dedicated to everyone who has helped me on my journey. Thank you. Now I can turn and strengthen my brothers and sisters.

THE JOG

My grace is su-ffi-cient. As I breathed in deeply, the crisp November air chilled my nose. Lungs expanding, the invigorating wintry air woke up every part of me. Working harmoniously with my heartbeat and my stride, my lungs breathed in what was needed, then exhaled what was not needed. The graceful rhythmic patterns of breathing helped me maintain my pace. My body, even though it held the cold air for only seconds, warmed it, then sent it back to the world. My nose was grateful for the returning warmth.

As I breathed in the chilly air then exhaled it

during my morning jog, I looked forward to the upcoming holidays. Family, friends, cooking, time off of work, gift exchanges. Jogging opens a different part of me. It allows me space to dream and plan. Imagine and create. Reflect and learn. The upcoming gathering of family and friends would be in my home. I was mentally creating the atmosphere for a day that hadn't yet come. *If I decorate the tree with a burlap-and-berries theme this year, I could coordinate that with the new place mats I got. I'll play that new music I found online, and light the peppermint candle I just bought, and...*It was all coming together. I was setting the atmosphere.

I've enjoyed running as far back as I can remember. Fifth grade was my first opportunity to run in a track meet. Late spring in Minneapolis was beautiful—great weather for sitting on a blanket in the cool grass while eating snacks, hanging out with friends in between track events. Placing in most events I competed in brought happiness. Bringing home ribbons and trophies after each meet to show my parents kept a smile on my face for days. Running was joy.

Now, there are no track meets. No

competitions or trophies. But, I still run. It's what I do to live more fully. When I jog, the logical part of my mind settles and gives way to the creative part of me. I can sense God more easily. I can hear things within myself that don't often get opportunity to surface during a typical work day.

What surfaced during this November jog was a memory from years prior. Ten years prior. It was a pressing time where I was treated less than my worth by leaders in a church. I was ready to leave, but leaving wasn't an immediate option. Paychecks were tied to that church, and no other jobs were open at the time. I had to stay, endure, and allow myself to internally be okay, even though externally it was not okay. Even though I wanted to escape this situation, I knew I had to remain there until another door opened.

Church hurt. Mega-church hurt, actually. God required me to remain there and endure. The pressure felt so intense. Oppressive. I couldn't see it at the time, but now I can see that God was showing me that it is possible to live in peace, even in the midst of pressure and confusion—that He could be trusted even when He didn't directly answer my questions.

Going through this pressing time created questions in me. *Where was God in all of this? Why would He allow leaders of His church to treat others like they did—like usable commodities for their own purposes? I thought this was* ministry. *Why?*

It had been a time of confusion, not knowing where to put my trust, not understanding why God was allowing certain things to happen, feeling trapped. The only words I heard the Lord say during this time came when I would jog. As my feet would meet the pavement, with each step, in tempo I'd hear, *My. Grace. Is. Su-ffi-cient.*

Back then, that seemed a little unfair of God to leave it at that. That's all He would tell me. I wanted Him to tell me He was about to move me somewhere else. I wanted Him to make His *other children* act right. I expected Him to speak to me in church, or when I prayed. But He didn't speak the words I thought I needed, nor did He speak in the places I expected Him to. But when I jogged He spoke in cadence with what He knew I needed. *My. Grace. Is. Su-ffi-cient.*

I didn't understand how powerful His grace actually is. *Now,* I understand that His grace is more than enough to see me through everything that will ever come my way.

Recounting how God turned that situation into something that worked for my good caused thankfulness to flow from my heart towards God. The cold air filled my lungs and brought a sense of refreshing as my feet moved me forward. *That was a rough one, Lord. Thank you for seeing me through that, and for blessing me with the career and church family that I have now. Your. Grace. Is. Su-ffi-cient! BIRD?!*

My pace was unexpectedly thrown off-beat as a bird flew right in front of me—eye level. I would've run right into it had I not side-stepped off my path. *Why was it flying so low? Was it injured? How did it not see me?* The out-of-place bird fluttered its wings, then began to gain height as it flew away. Then it was out of sight. Gone.

Your. Grace. Is. Su-ffi-cient. As I got my jogging rhythm back, my imagination kicked in and somehow connected my reflections to the bird. In my mind's eye, I saw a caged bird. The cage was large enough that the bird had enough space to move, but it was still caged. Locked in. Confined. Then, the cage door opened and the bird left the cage. It flew away. Freedom! That was me.

I had felt trapped during that season ten years prior, but then suddenly set free. I reflected how from one day to the next, a door had opened and it all changed. New city, new job, new church, new friends. Newness was what I was living in *now*. My jogging pace quickened as thankfulness turned to joy at the realization that God truly had opened a door of escape for me out of that situation so many years ago.

When I jog, I pace myself to a rhythm. On this morning, the "my-grace-is-su-ffi-cient" phrase kept me on pace. And then I started hearing other phrases. *Live in liberty. You've been set free. I give joy for sorrow.* The phrases were coming like rapid fire—I started running faster to keep up! I was so excited to get home and write these down. *Was it a song? A poem, maybe?* When I finally got home I grabbed a notebook and began writing. *Opened* was written in the next few moments.

Opened

Lord, I'm tired of this struggle. Things don't seem right. I feel closed in.

But, when You say it's my time, this trouble will be over...but until then...

I'll trust Your grace to keep me, Your spirit to lead me…to a place where I can say…

Opened, a captives been set free.

Opened, to live in liberty.

You've given joy for sorrow and hope for tomorrow. Opened.

On the other side of trouble, it's easier to see just what God had planned.

All the hurt and the pain, I'll count it all for gain. It was then I learned to worship You.

The feelings deep inside, the tears I cried, it's all right here in this alabaster box.

I will open, pour out to worship You.

Open, no matter what cost I have to go through.

You've given joy for sorrow and hope for tomorrow. Opened!

These words stayed in my journal, which stayed in my night stand drawer, which remained unopened for a while. A few years passed. Like the bird that came out of nowhere, I didn't see what was about to cross my path. It was out of place. It was lower than it should've been. It didn't belong in my life. I would have to side-step many times to keep from running into things that weren't supposed to be in my path. It would be a time of deep suffering—the battle of my life. It would cause me to lose my rhythm for many miles to come.

Never dreaming that I would face divorce, I was numb from shock for months. Confusion coupled with depression tried to take over and wreck my mind. I went back to the words of *Opened* for comfort—thinking that if God brought me out of my past confusion, surely He could do something about what I was facing now. Granted, there was no comparison of the measure of hurt between the situations. But I was desperately trying to find something to soothe the pain.

David encouraged Himself in the Lord with Psalms. I was trying to do the same. The words of *Opened* had been written, but the music had not yet come to me. I'd make up melodies and sing the words to myself while driving. I played them on my saxophone when I was alone. I'd soon realize that the music to *Opened* was being written right in the middle of my deepest pain.

When we experience pain, sometimes the

battle in our minds can make the situation even more intense. Worry and fear can overtake our thoughts and make us feel afraid or anxious. Being delivered from negative thoughts and emotions requires a mental discipline to stay focused on truth. My deliverance came from learning what God said about me.

For every fearful thought I had, I would search for a scripture or positive thought to combat it. When I felt hopeless, I claimed the promise that all things were working for my good. When the tears flowed, I remembered that God said He bottles my tears, and that when I cry to Him, He causes my enemies to turn back. When I didn't think I could take another minute of what life was dealing me, I spoke out loud, "I walk in the strength of the Lord." Promises are available to us in the Bible. We must believe. But, in order to believe, first we have to *know.*

I'm a pastor's kid. Raised in church. Most family members are in some type of formal ministry. High expectations. God-stuff was what we did, who we were, what we talked about. So much so, that I never really had to look too far to learn about spiritual things growing up. It was just always there for the taking. But now…Now was different. Now was gut-wrenching. Where was God *now*?

Until this point in my life, I had never really studied the Bible. I read it out of duty. I believed it. But I never *searched* for truth from it. When the intensity of pain overwhelmed me, I was desperate for help. I realized I needed something beyond human capability while sitting in my grandparent's living room.

I remember looking around at loving family members and seeing strength, support, care—it was all there as it had always been. I looked around, wondering who I could talk to for help. *My aunt? Grandma? Can anyone take this pain away?* The realization that nobody in this room, *in any room*, could help calm the pain in me brought panic. Humanity wasn't able to help. That left God. *Was God enough to take away this pain?* I didn't yet know but would soon find out. He is.

Some days I felt hopeful about my future as God would breathe life back into my being. Those were good days. Other days the dread of facing *more* was so heavy that I asked God to just take me. The pain was beyond what I felt I could bear.

I remember waking up one morning disappointed that I had lived through the night, because I thought that meant another day of pain awaited me. And yet, God was there every day. I don't know why He didn't just lift things off of me. I saw Him do that for others. I couldn't seem to reach healing as fast as others did. They would be the ones bringing home the ribbons and trophies this time.

In the struggle, I was learning that His grace was sufficient to lead me forward, even if the heaviness remained. The lessons He taught me during this time remain with me for eternity. Priceless relationship-building time between me and my Creator. I was learning to remain in Him, learning how to give Him my heart and my stride.

I was learning to breath in what was needed, then breath out and exhale what was not needed. Like my body that took in cold air, warmed it, then returned it to the world, I was taking in the bitter coldness of rejection, and asking God to allow me to feel the warmth of His love so I could return goodness to the world around me. God is in us, even when it doesn't feel like it. When we are weak, He remains strong.

Endure whatever you are facing. If it's confusion, pressure, pain or whatever other suffering there is, He can make it to be okay within you because *He is in you*. We will never be able to control what happens to us. But we are always in control of how we respond. It probably will never *feel* okay. But it can be. God is working on your behalf. Nobody masters the art of always responding correctly. Don't be too hard on yourself if you try and fail. Keep trying. As we do our best to act in obedience, He works with us.

Ask Him for help, for direction, for whatever you need. Then listen. Let Him answer. Breathe in deeply when He answers. Let your lungs fill with His presence—peace, identity, security, hope, joy, love. He is the breath of life. Breathe in as much as you can. Then exhale what does not belong to you— unforgiveness, impatience, hatred, revenge.

He speaks in many different ways. Tune in. Take time to discover how and where you hear Him best. Maybe it's listening to certain types of music, heading to the coast for a day, making sure you are eating and resting properly, or simply taking a little time in the midst of a busy schedule and asking Him to help you get things right! Our lives are so full of distractions that most times we don't even hear Him speaking, yet He still speaks. He desires to be your very breath, your source of life, whatever you need whenever you need it.

You *can* endure. He can take brokenness and turn it into blessing if you will allow Him to take you through the process. The process. It's hard. Stay in it. I may never understand His timing, or choice of allowances into my life, and I know I'll always have unanswered questions. But above all of that, I know He is a good Father and He will finish what He starts. He began the good work and will be faithful to complete it!

As God brought me through the battlefield of divorce, I knew He was requiring a certain sound from me. Namely, the words that would come from my mouth. I *felt* like speaking words of revenge, accusation, or words that would at least defend my reputation. But that was not what He wanted.

When we suffer, it's tempting to seek attention and let the world around us know just how bad we have it by complaining or retelling our sorrows. But the purpose of suffering is not to draw attention to ourselves. It's to grow us, stretch us, to mature us, to deepen our capacity for more of Him.

Of course it's okay to talk to others who can help guide us through our suffering. Mentoring friendships are a God-send. Just check your intentions. Are you seeking help, or attention? Wanting to complain, or willing to get wise counsel?

I knew I was being delivered. I knew God was transforming me. I journaled most nights and found writing to be therapeutic. So much so, that I contemplated writing a book. But, I knew there was still bitterness in me. So I put the book away. I didn't write for many years to come as I kept working through brokenness. What I *did* do was study Isaiah. Why Isaiah? Because there was a verse that caught my attention.

Water has always been special to me. I have sentimental memories of walking along the river in my grandparent's backyard, joyful memories of spending summers laughing with high school friends at the pool, bonding memories of fishing with my family at Minnesota lakes, peaceful memories of spending time at the Florida coast, and awe-struck memories of Caribbean ocean water that seems to have a life all of its own.

There are also memories of fear from Louisiana hurricanes dumping thousands of gallons of water on us, and memories of panic as Texas hail destroyed our cars and home. But let's stick to the positive memories of water!

Each type of water elicits a different memory for me. I think God created water that way. It's one element, but it serves different purposes. God has a way of using water.

HEALING WATERS

I am not a Bible scholar by any means. I am just someone who got hungry enough to dig deep until I found what I was looking for. For several months I studied Isaiah 41. Its reference to water intrigued me. As I pulled apart the meaning of each word in these verses, I could not believe what was uncovered. It amazed me how these scriptures, written so long ago, were speaking directly to me in specific ways. Challenged by how to present this in book form, I decided to share it with you just how I got it—word by word.

Isaiah 41:17 says, "When the poor and needy seek water and there is none, and their tongue faileth for thirst, I the Lord will hear them, I the God of Israel will not forsake them."

When the poor and needy seek water

The word *poor* means to be depressed in one's mind or in one's circumstance, to be afflicted, defenseless, browbeaten, or to be looked down upon and pressed. It depicts a powerful lawless person mistreating the defenseless person through oppression. The mistreatment creates a cycle that becomes more intense over time. The oppressed people become increasingly weakened, which gives the oppressor even more control over them. And the cycle gets more extreme over time.

The reference goes back to when Israel was told not to withhold wages from servants because the servants were poor, *ani*. Israel was instructed to let these people glean, let them have at least the leftovers. Israel was warned not to afflict these people because all they had left was hope to make it one more day, if they even had that. They owned nothing. They had no rights. They were completely dependent on the welfare of others. Oppressed. Poor.

Have you been there? If you have, then you

know you don't get there in a day. Oppression will stick around a long time and try to wear you out. It happens so slowly that it's hard to recognize from one day to the next. First, maybe it's a bad day. Then, a melancholy week. Then, a pessimistic attitude. If you don't catch it, before you know it your joy and strength are gone and it feels like nothing will *ever* get better. But God says He will hear you and He will not forsake you. He will help you break free from whatever oppression you may be facing.

The word *needy* means to want—especially in one's emotions. It also means to breathe after, or to long for. It comes from the word *ebyon*, which pictures people who are in lack because they lost their possessions. It is also used to describe those who need protection and who cry out to God as their source. In this verse, the needy person is completely desperate for something that only God can give. Oppressed. Emotionally spent. Poor. Desperate.

The word *seek* means to strive after, to desire earnestly. It comes from the word *baqash,* which is a picture of God seeking us. When God sought us, it required Him sacrificing His Son. That's intense seeking. It is also a picture of us seeking God. Our seeking Him should be intense. Seeking requires sacrifice. Seeking is not half-hearted, nor can it be done with an I'll-do-it-as-time-allows attitude. Seeking has to be a whole-hearted desire. It costs. But as we learn to seek Him, the desire for more of Him grows in us, and it becomes easier to give more of ourselves to Him and His purpose.

Water represents a refreshing. In general, water is an element that is essential for life. It comes from the word *may*. God made water. He controls the boundaries of water. He appoints springs to break forth. He causes rain to fall. He is concerned with the flow of rivers. Water is given as a sign of blessing from God. It also symbolizes inner purity. Jesus even referred to Himself as water—water that would quench our every thirst.

Their tongue faileth for thirst

The word *tongue* has to do with one's speech. It is from the root word *lashon*. This person's tongue would normally be used for speaking life (Proverbs 18:21), and wisdom and kindness (Proverbs 31:26). The tongue of a righteous person is regarded as fine silver (Proverbs 10:20). But, because this verse is talking about the needy—those who are desperately crying out to God—it indicates that something has happened to their speech. It has failed.

To have a tongue that fails means the tongue isn't functioning in its purpose. The tongue was created with a purpose to speak blessings. But here, the tongue isn't speaking life. Maybe it used to be able to speak life-giving words, but something happened to the tongue in this verse, and now life is not coming forth. The ability to speak life, blessing, and encouragement has been taken. Thirst has caused the tongue to fail, which has caused life to cease.

To thirst means to not only be thirsty, but to experience suffering because the thirst has been there for so long. It comes from the root word *sama*, which pictures a besieged city's water supply getting cut off. Imagine being in a city, forced to ration what little water you have left. *Will my children get to drink today?*

Imagine watching your children endure suffering, and probably intense pain from having no water. Not only was there the issue of being thirsty, but the lack of water created a myriad of other issues that brought pain and disease. Dealing with suffering *without* being thirsty is difficult enough. But, enduring suffering while not having a basic need being met is even tougher. Besieged. Under attack. No water. Thirsty.

I the Lord will hear them

When God says He will hear us, it means He will respond because He has been paying attention to us. It connects back to the word *ana*, which means to answer. God doesn't have to answer us, but out of His mercy and compassion He does. God pays attention. God answers. Sometimes it *feels* as if His back is turned and He has no idea what we go through. Because how could a loving God knowingly allow suffering to continue in our lives? Why doesn't He do something about it?

The *easy* answer is that He does see. He is doing something about it. He does answer. *Easy* because it's easy to write that. I don't have to explain why, why not, how long, what if, or get into the unanswerable questions of the heart. That answer is *easy* because it's nicely packaged, generalizable to any situation. *Challenging* because what we see with our eyes rarely makes those answers go down easily. Our natural senses take in information that usually goes against the belief that

God is working all things out for my good.

How is church hurt good for me? How is a divorce good for me? How is your pain good for you? Church hurt, divorce, or whatever catastrophe or pain you face, is *not* good within itself. It's wrong to be mistreated. God has given humanity free-will that even He doesn't override. He lets us choose. People have free-wills and sometimes choose to hurt others.

But, if you respond right, you can become better on the other side of suffering. Keep in mind, bad things don't come from God. It is not God's design for bad things to happen to us. But, He will allow us to suffer to perfect our faith. He will use every event we face to perfect us. So be assured, He does hear us and He is working. We must endure the process.

Once we settle within ourselves that He does see and is answering, there is a response. In this verse, the response that is associated with this word *ana* is singing. Singing is the natural human response to being heard by God!

I, the God of Israel, will not forsake them.

Forsake means to loosen one's grip or to

leave destitute. It comes from the word *azab,* which means to abandon, neglect, or put aside. How comforting to know that God will never brush us off. He is faithful. Most times, He does not answer how we think He should, or when we think He should. But, that doesn't mean He hasn't heard. It doesn't mean He's not answering.

Worry and anxiety diminish when we learn to trust Him, His timing, His answers or seemingly lack of answering in our lives. Maybe you've heard the expression *every event in your life is either God-sent or God-used*, and that *if He didn't send it, He can still use it*. And, *everything that we experience gets filtered through the hands of a loving God*. It doesn't always feel that way. How could a loving God allow this or that?

There are Theological debates around that very question. I don't have the deepest Theologically sound answer on that one. But, I do know that God doesn't need my explaining His reasons for doing what He does. He doesn't need me to defend His God-hood—as if my mortal explanations could add anything to an immortal God, or my lack of explanation have the ability to detract from His reputation. He doesn't need me to defend Him. He is God. He does what He will. I can't explain His doings. But I trust Him. After walking through fires that burned away so much of me yet left much of Him, I trust His love for me. I believe more now than ever that whatever comes my way can be used for my eternal good, if I let Him help me respond.

Romans 8:28 says, "And we know that all things work together for the good to them that love God, to them who are the called according to His purpose." You can be free from the pressure of trying to figure out what God is doing. Be free from the pressure of trying to make things work out on your own. Know that every event that happens to you, good or bad, is working for your eventual good.

Let's put it all together. Here's a paraphrase: When you cry and aren't being taken care of, when you become depressed in your mind and in your spirit, when no one is protecting you, and you have been left in want...When you cry out for help with everything you have, when you strive for the one thing that you think will meet your need and quench your thirst but it's not there—it's not that it's there and you can't find it, it's just not there at all...when you've experienced dryness for so long that you can't even speak a word of encouragement over yourself because of the suffering you've been through, God hears you. *Even though you can't speak, God hears you.* He pays close attention to you with an earnest intent of helping you. He watches over you with compassion. The God of Israel will not lose you. He has a tight firm grip on you and will never throw you away. You are forever in His hand and nobody can take you out. He will not allow this condition to be your conclusion. He will not abandon you.

Here's what He will do for you. Isaiah 41:18 says, "I will open rivers in high places and fountains in the midst of valleys. I will make the wilderness a pool of water and the dry land springs of water, that they may see and know that the hand of the Lord has done this."

I will open rivers in high places

To *open* means to unstop, to plow through, to break forth, and to set free. It comes from the root word *patah,* which means to liberate, to open one's mouth, to carve or engrave. When you open your mouth to speak, you are engraving your own future. Your words act like a massive chisel that is forging a path for a river, your life, to follow after.

What you speak really does have an impact on your life. Find out what the Bible says and begin to speak that over yourself and those around you. Open your mouth, speak life and break through to freedom.

Remember from verse 17, the tongue failed because of dryness? But here, God says He will open the mouth so life can break forth! God will break through the oppression and liberate us to speak life again!

The words we speak are so important. Proverbs 18:21 teaches that life and death are in the power of the tongue. Be aware of what you say. Practice saying what the Word says about your situation. Don't allow yourself to get to that place where you're so thirsty and dry that you can't even speak a word of encouragement to yourself. Choose to speak life!

The word *river* represents something that sparkles, something that is cheerful. A river has a flow to it. The fact that it flows implies that there is movement, that things are progressing. Don't become stagnant. Things rot in stagnation. Keep speaking life until your flow and sparkle come back.

Places is a word associated with a

household, a family, or people that are close to you. It represents something or someone on the inside.

This phrase tells us that God wants to break through things that have previously represented barriers to us. Our role is to come into agreement with His word. He wants us to break forth in our families, in our closest relationships. He said He would plow through barriers and strongholds, especially as they relate to our homes. He has given us the gift of language to initiate this movement and to help us keep progressing. Speak life!

Family issues are tough. My family issue was divorce. Twice. Nothing makes me want to withdraw and stop speaking life faster than pain in my closest relationships. So as I studied this, I shook my head as if to tell God, "Are you serious? You expect me to speak life right now?" But I did it anyway, out of obedience and faith that if He was showing me in Isaiah to do something, I better do it.

I didn't do it perfectly. I still don't. But I'm getting better. I'm glad I chose back then to obey. I spoke life to my young son, right in the midst of our greatest pain. Even though I was hurting deeply, I still spoke encouragement and life to my son. God used my words to bring healing to the one closest to me.

Fountains in the midst of valleys

The word *fountains* stems from the word *mayan,* which means a source of satisfaction, a well or spring. It's something that has the ability to refresh. *Valleys* represent division. Visualize two mountains next to each other with a deep valley between them. The valley is the location where the mountains are separated, breaking apart from one another. Valleys are places of ripping, a breach, or a tear.

Have you ever had a relationship, or a job, or some form of stability ripped from you? It hurts. God says that in the torn places He will bring a source of satisfaction. While studying this, I could not imagine how it would ever be possible to experience anything that would satisfy me while I was in the valley, the ripped apart place.

I remember praying, "How Lord? What could You possibly do to make me feel satisfied in this valley? I don't have anything left to work with. Everything I expected out of life has been torn from me. My whole life is shattered, and You're telling me I am going to be satisfied?"

Being satisfied wasn't an instant thing, but it did come. God would speak the phrase *fountains in the midst of valleys* to me every day until I decided to believe it. Then, new opportunities began to come to me which resulted in joy because they were in line with my purpose. God knew what to set before me to get my attention.

He knows what truly satisfies us, because He created us. He designed us. God knew, way better than I did, what He placed on the inside of me that could be ignited in purpose, even if I were in a valley. He knows how to open a fountain in the middle of a valley!

I will make the wilderness a pool of water

The root word for wilderness is *midbar*, the place of no water and the place where no pleasant thing dwells. Another meaning has to do with words being spoken. Researching further gave a picture of cattle being driven. This wilderness represents a place where one is being directed through speech, a place where one has been driven by someone else's words. It's being controlled and manipulated.

Picture the cattle. They don't get to walk wherever they want to. They are not free. They are forced to go where the rancher wants them to go. Can you relate? Have you felt driven by someone else's words over you? Good things can't grow in us when we are being controlled by someone else.

I had to learn not to allow other people's voices to occupy my mind. It can become overwhelming when you listen to too many opinions. Or maybe it's not that there are so many voices. Perhaps it's just one voice that repeatedly speaks, "You're never going to make it. You're not good enough." Have you been driven by someone's words to you?

God says He will make this wilderness a pool of water. Think about the water in a pool. It's collected. Calm. Peaceful. A pool doesn't have crashing waves like the ocean. Pools don't flow like a river, or suddenly spring up like a fountain. Pools are still. Be still and know that He is God.

God wants to silence any tormenting voices you are hearing. He wants your spirit to be at peace. Stilled. Quieted with His love. He wants your mind and your spirit to be calm and collected, not wild and driven.

I will make the dry land springs of water

Dry means to be barren or alone. It comes from the word *siya,* which means dryness or drought. Barrenness, feeling like we're never going to produce anything, can make us feel dried up. Aloneness...Feeling alone is isolating. It leads to despair. Drought.

A *spring* represents being brought out. It relates to the rising of the sun, the beginning of a new day, growth, or the beginning of a new thing. It stems from the word *mosa*, which means a place of going out. A spring indicates that there is something good lying deep within that has to come out quickly.

How awesome to know that God wants to take our barrenness and dryness and create new life. We all have things inside of us that God wants to bring out of us. There are relationships He intends for us to have to bring us new life, opportunities He designed for us to experience that will cause us to produce. Sometimes it takes going through these dry lands to get all of that out of us.

Paraphrasing this verse could read like this: I will break through barriers and set you free to be light-hearted within yourself and among your close connections. In the place where you've been torn, ripped, or broken, I will create a source of satisfaction. Where you've been driven like an animal in your mind because of someone's words to you, I will make you to be still, peaceful, and collected. And in the places where there's been no life or joy, I will create a new thing in you. I will cause the sun to rise quickly and I will create a new day for you. I do this so you will see and know that My hand is on your life. I am with you.

PLANTING TREES

In the next verse it says, "I will plant in the wilderness the cedar and shittah tree, and the myrtle tree, and the oil tree. I will set in the desert the fir tree, and the pine and the box tree together." (Isaiah 41:19)

I will plant in the wilderness the cedar and shittah tree

When God says He will *plant*, it means He will give, restore, trade, or grant a request to. The word *plant* comes from the word *natan,* which pictures a hand reaching out to give. Every good gift comes from God. He is reaching toward us to bring restoration. God's hand reaches to us, ready to give.

The wilderness mentioned in this verse is the same wilderness as in the previous verse—the place where someone is driven in his or her mind.

The cedar tree is known for having tenacious roots. It is connected to the word *erez*, which provides more insight about these trees. They grow best in high, dry regions. They spread their roots among the rocks so as to secure a stronghold. (Strongholds can be good or bad. A stronghold is anything that has enough strength to have and maintain control.) This tree knows how to dig deep. It's not a here-today-gone-tomorrow kind of tree. This cedar is mighty.

Cedars also produce an oil that prevents destruction. It's known for its strength and also its ability to produce something that prevents the destruction of others.

We are called to be high and not low, above only and not beneath. God intends for us to live above our circumstances instead of getting all twisted up in them. Rise above.

We are to spread our roots so deep that a mighty stronghold of God is established in us—so deep that it doesn't matter what circumstance we face. We will be so securely rooted that nothing can take us out. Rooted and grounded in love. Our roots are to be so strong that others can't help but be affected by us—so strong that we prevent those around us from being destroyed. We become a refuge for others because of our tenacious root system of strength.

The shittah tree is related to the acacia tree, an impenetrable tree. The shittah traces back to words that have to do with building a family, repairing what has been damaged, or obtaining children. God is interested in healthy families. His first institution on the earth was the family.

In our day, there are not many healthy images of family life. Our families need repair. We need to be restored to God's purpose for the family. When our families are intact, there is an impenetrable tree. There is a place of safety for spouses and children when the family is healthy.

The myrtle tree, and the oil tree

This next tree symbolizes so much in scripture that there could be entire books written on it. The myrtle tree is an evergreen that grows in the desert. It was first recognized at Ghizan, a place so dry that it is called *Techama*, which means hell.

Staying green in a desert—staying alive while you go through hell—that's the myrtle. That's you. In the wilderness that feels like hell, God wants to plant in us the ability to stay green. He wants us to flourish right in the midst of it all. The surroundings that would kill other plants somehow doesn't kill the myrtle. The circumstances that have taken others out will not take you out.

A myrtle tree produces myrrh, a substance that is bitter to taste but sweet to smell. In order to get the myrrh from the tree, the bark has to be broken and wounded, forming large cavities that become filled with granular secretions. The words *wounded* and *bleed* are actually used to describe the process of harvesting the oil from the myrrh tree.

The myrtle tree is wounded for the purpose of bleeding. The harvesters job is to make the myrtle bleed because what's on the inside is so valuable. The sap and resin that get excreted from this tree is used for healing wounds. The myrrh gets *wounded* to the point of *bleeding* so it can bring healing to others' wounds. What a beautiful analogy of Jesus' death on the cross. What a beautiful analogy of His work in your life.

It is one of the few components that can heal without causing side effects. It stimulates the production of white blood cells, which are used to fight infections. Myrrh increases the appetite and promotes the absorption and assimilation of nutrition. In deficient or excessive conditions, myrrh restores the normal conditions.

If you're going through what seems comparable to hell on earth right now, know that God can use this to get something out of you that will be so valuable it will bring healing not only to you, but also to the people around you. You are being wounded. Being broken hurts. But what's on the inside of you, the Christ part of you, is flowing out. Only when the myrtle is broken can the healing properties come forth.

There is value coming out of you as a result of this situation. That doesn't even make sense while you're enduring suffering. You should be dead in this wilderness. You should be bruised so badly that no good thing should flow from your life. How could any good thing come out of this hell? But remember, God is planting the evergreen myrtle in you. God is restoring balance back to your life.

Myrrh is bitter to the taste. If you taste your surroundings, it's going to be bitter. If you become bitter in the suffering, you're going to poison yourself and those around you. You'll become a disease when you were supposed to be the cure for the disease. Let no bitterness take root in you, because it will come back out of you and defile many. Exhale the bitterness. It does not belong to you.

Myrrh is sweet to smell. Perfume. Your life is supposed to have the aroma of Christ. When you reject bitterness, you receive a blessing. Even when there is bitterness all around you, don't take it in. Reject it, and watch what God will do inside of you. He will bring health, balance, increase your appetite for life, restore, and bring wholeness *with no side effects*. He will bless you with His aroma in your life. Sweetness.

Oil represents richness, the anointing, and fruitfulness. Oil comes from the word *shemen,* which symbolizes the rich blessing and prosperity of God. In Deuteronomy 32:13 the rocks, that which normally gives no blessing, gave honey and oil under God's command. In Isaiah 61:3 it says that

God will trade the oil of joy for our mourning. In both of these verses, God is trading what He has for what we have. He takes our hardness, dryness and mourning, and gives us sweet joy and blessing, prosperity and health. Why wouldn't we trade?

A paraphrase for the first part of this verse could read like this: In the wilderness—the dry place where you have been controlled or driven, God will plant in you a tenacity to make it through the drought. He will create an inner root system in you that will be so strong and deep, it will be a stronghold the enemy can't shake. You will be impenetrable. Instead of someone else having a stronghold over you, now God has fortified you with His strength, and He will produce something in you of great value. And, when you get hurt He will not only heal you, but also allow what you go through to be used to help others. What should have destroyed you will actually be God's vehicle to bring His blessing to you. The place that should have dried you up will instead be the place where you make the great exchange with God—beauty for ashes, gladness for mourning, praise for heaviness. When you make the trade, there will be blessing instead of bitterness.

I will set in the desert the fir tree, and the pine and the box tree together.

The desert spoken of here means to be covered like at dusk, and to mingle like the strands of a braid. It comes from the word *araba*, which means a plain, step, or plateau. It's as if someone was living life enthusiastically, things were going pretty good, then the darkness began to set in and cover him. It got harder to keep producing at the level he was used to. It used to be morning, and everything was fresh and new and growing. But now the darkness has set in, and it's hard to even see. The drought has come and things aren't growing as fast as they used to. Growth has seemingly reached its plateau. Life is as good as it will ever be.

When you get covered with dusk-ness, be careful not to get braided or intertwined with distractions. It's easy to mingle in things we're not supposed to when what used to work doesn't work anymore. If your growth has seemed to reach a plateau, don't worry. It won't stay this way forever. Stay focused and take this time to dig your roots even deeper. Wait on the Lord to bring you through this and allow your strength to be renewed. Go back to what you know to be true. Study and dig in the

Word until you find what you need. Don't settle for plateau living when you can climb higher. There's more for you. God's answer for the desert is the fir, pine, and box tree.

The fir tree was used to make musical instruments in the Old Testament. It is also an evergreen. The fir tree is referenced in Isaiah 37:24, which describes there being a time of restitution—instead of thorns, fir trees come up. Meaning, instead of pain, there is music. When God says it's time for you to receive restitution for all the enemy has done to you, there will be a joy that comes out of you. No more painful thorns—it's time to pull out the musical instruments! Don't level off and accept the plateau. This is *not* as good as it gets. God always has more for us than we can imagine.

The pine tree is known for being a hard, strong, enduring, lasting tree. The pine tree comes from a word that means to pause. When you're in a strong position you can afford to pause before acting. You can take time to pause, to pray. You have an advantage over your opponent when you're in a strong position. There is no panic and anxiety to make rushed decisions. You don't have to make something happen when you're sure that everything is going to be alright. Strength allows for time to pause. Endure your situation and pause until you hear His counsel. That's how you will last.

The box tree is a type of cedar tree that is known for standing straight. It symbolizes being level, honest, happy, and blessed. It is from the word *tashshur*, which means to walk in the way of understanding. *Straight* implies integrity. Being honest and straight with God, ourselves, and others is what God requires. No deception. No fraud. When we stand straight we can be sure that God will back us up. There is a blessing that comes from walking with integrity.

Together means at the same time. All of these trees get planted *together*—next to, simultaneously, all at the same time. God won't make you choose which tree you want. He is a giver of all good things and says that He will plant all of these trees *together*!

Together, all at the same time, you can experience tenacious strength that allows you to flourish even in hard, dry seasons. In drought, you can remain green and be repaired. You can be assured that there's more in store for you—no levelling off and getting distracted. Together—all at the same time—choose to be joyful, sing, know that you have time to pause, pray, choose to live a life of integrity. All at the same time.

A paraphrase for the last part of the verse could read: In that place where you've been covered up with something that has caused you to slow down and maybe even settle for less (keep in mind you weren't always this way but something happened and you've leveled off like a plateau)...In that place where you know there's more but you can't seem to produce anything, God says He will put a song there. The last thing anybody wants to do when they're not producing is to sing. But, praise is a powerful tool. God created praise to open things. He gives us praise as an opportunity to get out of where we are.

In the desert, the place you don't want to stay because it seems like nothing is getting accomplished, He will enable you to endure and have life abundantly, green. When you are still and endure, God will go to work and build character in you so you can stand straight in integrity. You will become strong like the pine tree—strong enough and confident enough in God to be able to trust Him and wait for His timing and direction. So be patient, even when it seems like nothing is being done. God is planting His trees in you. He is bringing all of this together.

Waiting

James 1:3-4 says, "Let patience have her perfect work, that ye may be perfect and entire, wanting nothing." God wants us to endure our daily situations while trusting Him to work in our life. While we look to Him, He works on our behalf, puts pieces back together the way He wants them to be.

What does that look like? How do we go through that kind of process? With patience. But to get to patience we have to endure. With trust. To get to trust we have to believe He is a loving God and has our best in mind. Sometimes that's so hard. But it really comes down to us choosing. It's a choice. It's faith.

When we choose faith, God works on our behalf and we become perfected. Perfect and flawless? Never. We become perfect in the sense that we lack nothing at the end of that particular trial. We learned the lesson, passed that test, and move on to the next one. When we remain in Him through the suffering we will ultimately get to the place where we are in want of nothing!

Isaiah 40:31 says, "They that wait upon the Lord shall renew their strength. They shall run and not get weary, they shall walk and not faint." If we *don't* wait and listen for God's direction, we'll get weary. If you don't wait on the Lord, your strength won't be renewed. When you run, you're going to get tired. And when you walk, you're going to faint. You'll stay in the desert place allowing distractions in, chasing busy-ness trying to make things happen, all the while getting nowhere.

Somehow we think that if we're busy, then we're accomplishing something. Maybe, but not necessarily. It would be more beneficial to put aside the busy-ness and ask God what He has for us. Be patient and allow patience to work in you so that you can get to that strong place and be in need of nothing. Pause.

Before I learned to sit still and wait, I thought I was supposed to fight everything that hit me. That is exhausting! I was so weak from fighting back all of the time because I thought every battle was mine. Now that I've learned a *little* bit better to wait and allow my strength to be renewed, I am a *little* more patient with life and as a result I feel stronger.

Life hasn't slowed down any. It's actually become more involved. I deal with just as much now, if not more. But, it doesn't feel like it because God has strengthened me on the inside. I don't have to react to everything that comes my way. When I take things to Him and wait on His response, He either takes care of it all by Himself or gives me a direction to go. *Be still and know that He is God.*

I have chosen faith enough times, seen God answer enough times that I am convinced. He didn't always answer like I wanted Him to, but He answered. As a result, my faith has been validated and I have become perfected from those trials. I still have more perfecting to experience. The more validated faith I have, the stronger my faith becomes. And this is the journey of life—the strengthening of our faith.

God wants you to be strong. He will give you joy so you can be strong. Nehemiah 8:10 says, "The joy of the Lord is your strength." If you don't feel strong, if you feel that oppressive dark cloud over you, like you're in that desert place, sing! No, you won't feel like singing. But sing in faith. He promised to give a garment of praise for the spirit of heaviness. Change your clothes—a heavy spirit for a royal robe of praise. When you sing to Him, God will inhabit your praise. Sing until you're strong! Then sing some more.

THE PROMISE

The next verse, Isaiah 41:20 says, "That they may see, and know, and consider, and understand together, that the hand of the LORD hath done this, and the Holy One of Israel hath created it."

That they may see, and know, and consider and understand together

To *see* means to have the ability to perceive, become aware, or to discern.

To *know* means to care, recognize, instruct, or designate. The word *know* comes from the word *yada,* which means to distinguish between what is beneficial and what is harmful. It requires experience and discernment to have a "knowing" as to whether something is beneficial or harmful.

For example, it doesn't seem that the loss of a job is beneficial when it happens. But, what if God is orchestrating a better job for you? What if He has a different career in mind for you that will lead you into your life's work? Every situation in your life can be used to further you into your purpose if you allow God to have His way *in* you. Recognize His working is beneficial for you.

The word *consider* comes from the word *sum,* which means to put in a location, to assign something to someone, to set aside for a special purpose or time, to appoint someone to a position, and to establish a new relationship. When God puts you somewhere, whether it be a geographical place or a season in life, He expects you to stay there until...

He has assigned you to be in that place for His purpose and only in His timing will that season end. Stay in it. Stay in it, and let it be okay. Staying can be so hard. But do it anyway. One of the results will be a deeper relationship with Him. Deep roots. You will learn an attribute of God that you've never experienced before. Faith. Trust. Love. Patience. Endurance. They all come from staying. Consider.

To understand has to do with your intelligence, or that which guides you. A person who has understanding will behave skillfully. Behaving skillfully is measured, thought-through, and takes practice. It also takes much discipline to control behavior. In Proverbs we are instructed to apply our hearts to understanding, but to lean not to our *own* understanding. We are to seek His perspective and adopt *that* understanding to our lives.

The root word for understand is *sakal*, which shows us the end result of behaving skillfully—being prudent. Being prudent brings success and prosperity.

This phrase has a lot to do with our inner workings, our thoughts, the way we view things that happen to us, how we interact with our world. To see, know, consider and understand all have implications for how we process what's going on around us, how we see life. God wants our seeing, knowing, and understanding to line up with His perspective so we can distinguish what is beneficial for us and what is not.

The hand of the lord hath done this

The word *hand* comes from the word *yawd,* which means to be opened. God is reaching to us with an open hand. *Yawd* also means power and direction, or to deliver. God is reaching toward us in power to give us direction and to deliver His promises to us.

The Holy One of Israel hath created this

Created comes from the root word *bara,* which has to do with the initiation of something. It also means to choose, to cut down because of being qualified to use, or to make fat. Once you go through your process, you become qualified to be used for the purpose He had in mind all along. It may feel like you are being cut down, but remember He disciplines those He loves. He chooses to use you when you allow suffering to have its purpose. He prunes us so we will produce much fruit. So much fruit that you are "fat"—you have extra, more than enough, exceeding abundant life.

God knows the end from the beginning. He has the end of a thing in mind before He begins. Have you ever considered that your days and times are in God's hands? That He is creating situations and tests for you to pass to get you precisely where He intended you to be before you were even born? Processes that have been strategically designed to get exactly what He wants to get out of you?

He is getting you ready for something bigger and better than what you're currently dealing with. Don't quit! Stay in there and go through the process. What's to come on the other side is beautiful!

Paraphrasing this verse could read: God will do all of this for you so that you will learn to view things as He does, so that you are able to recognize what is beneficial to you and what is not, so that you will be established in whatever place God decides to put you, so that you will learn to think and behave skillfully. God wants the best for you. He is working on your behalf to get you to the place that He originally designed for you to be. The place where you have more than enough. If you stay in the process you will get there.

Looking back at verses 17 through 20, there's so much God will do for us if we stay in the process and allow Him to have His way inside of us. I can understand wanting to quit because it seems hopeless…but not after reading these verses. As long as God is, there is hope.

If you are in the valley, God is offering you a way through it. He will take your brokenness, work with it, and you will come out of this with a life that is better than it was before it was broken. It'll be different. It may not be what you thought you wanted. But, He can transform and make all things new in a way that brings deep satisfaction. He will initiate this new thing in you. He has a purpose for your life and He will use everything you've been through to help fulfill that purpose.

Even if you've tried so many times before and failed, He will use that too. That's what is so awesome about God. Nothing in our lives goes to waste. Seemingly good or bad pasts don't matter as much as our present willingness to grow. He is able to redeem it all. He will gather up the pieces and recreate time and time again. Nobody is too far gone, too far spent, or too messed up for Him to work with. There is hope because there is God!

And He will perform all of these promises— break barriers, keep us in His hand, hear us with compassion, set us free, heal our families, bring us satisfaction, calm our minds, create deep joy in us, strengthen us and cause us to sing again! All of that just so we know He is God. So we know the hand of the Lord has done it. So we know that the holy One of Israel has worked this in us.

As much as we want to grow closer to Him, consider that He wants to be known! Consider all the specific ways He has promised to heal you, to bless you, to care for you. He desires relationship with you.

He is able to open whatever caged-in situation you find yourself in, and help you fly away. Freed. Healed. Blessed. *Opened*.

Lord, by Your spirit, go way down deep into our hearts and heal like only You can. Bring deliverance and liberty where there is bondage and oppression. Keep hope alive in us. Give us the strength and desire to enjoy life. Let your praise forever come forth from our tongues. Bring encouragement to keep us going through whatever process we are in. And when it gets tough, I thank you for the security that comes in knowing that You will never let go of us. Thank You for being faithful. Thank You that Your promises are forever true. Let us experience Your love in a special way. You are eternally good. There is nobody like You!

ABOUT THE AUTHOR

Heidi resides in San Antonio, Texas, where she is a math professor. Outside of work, Heidi enjoys spending time in nature, hanging out with friends, cooking, and eating chocolate. Her greatest joy is sharing life with her son, Ethan.

Heidi looks forward to the future with anticipation as God keeps expanding her horizons. The production of her saxophone instrumental CD, *Waves of Deliverance*, was her initial stepping beyond plateau living. The most recent project has been the writing of her book, *The Final Stretch*, which is a beautifully raw account of her life story as God led her through healing after experiencing crushing pain.

Health and wellness have been life themes for Heidi. She has experienced that through worship, working with the gifts God has given each of us, we can live in wholeness. Her desire is to see others healed and *working their gift*!

For information on other products, please visit
www.fullofhonor.com

95772022R00033

Made in the USA
Columbia, SC
21 May 2018